TIGER SALAMANDER

Unique Guide on Tiger Salamanders, their Care, Habitation, Caging, Feeding, and Lighting

Dr. Sarah Leonard

Table of Contents

CHAPTER 1

FOUNDATION OF TIGER SALAMANDERS

Tiger salamanders are the greatest land-based salamander.

Salamanders typically aren't at the pinnacle of the listing for most reptile and amphibian enthusiasts. They are considered as delicate, secretive and greater difficult to feed than frogs and now not very exact pets in general. And in the case of many salamander species, specifically some of the smaller ones, these are legitimate concerns. The tiger salamander, however, is none of the above, and it makes an excellent, hardy captive. It is likely the most interactive species of amphibian. The tiger salamander was, at one time, viewed a single species. Over the previous couple of decades, scientists diagnosed that it is countless intently associated species. These encompass the California tiger (Ambystoma californiense), the japanese tiger (A. tigrinum) and the Mexican tiger (A. velasci). There is additionally the barred tiger species complex, made up of various subspecies, together with the blotched tiger (A.

mavortium melanostictum) and the most placing of all tigers, the barred tiger salamander itself (A. mavortium mavortium). Tigers come in all manner of colors, from shiny creamy yellow stripes on a darkish brown or black background, to pure blue-gray, and even black with orange spots. Even inside races, the range of colours and markings can be shocking from character to individual. Some races are made up of populations of aquatic adults that seem to be very comparable to their shut relative the axolotl (A. mexicanum).

At eleven inches or larger, tigers

share the document for the greatest land-living salamander in the world with the large salamanders (Dicamptodon spp.). I've for my part viewed a 14-inch male, and there are information of even large aquatic adults. Tiger salamanders are located from the shores of the Atlantic to the Pacific coast of the continental United States, as nicely as southern Canada and a long way south into Mexico.

In fact, tigers are arguably extra sizeable than the American bullfrog (Rana catesbeiana), however whilst nearl

y all   of   us has considered a
bullfrog,   the   tiger   salamander
makes no noise and spends a lot of
time underground, so many by no
means understand they are there.
Tigers   are phase of
the crew acknowledged as   mole
salamanders.   They
are closely built,   with robust legs
and toes for   digging,
and quite small   eyes —
all true diversifications if   you
spend tons of
your lifestyles digging in the dirt.
Tiger salamanders adapt nicely to
captivity   with
the appropriate amphibian
supplies. Contrast this to the

similar-

looking noticed salamander, (A. maculatum), which is extraordinarily secretive and not often accepts meals at once from its keeper. Rarely, an person tiger stays stubbornly jumpy or standoffish; most lose their worry of human beings in time and end up relatively tame, leaping at fingers for meals and following their keepers from inside the terrarium. The everlasting smile-like expression on their faces is tough to resist. Sexually mature men have a tendency to be slim of build, have

flatter tails, and a
very surprisingly swollen cloaca
(the vent area, placed on
the backside of
the physique simply at the back
of the rear legs). A
mature girl is nicely rounded and
her cloaca is very small when in
contrast to that of the male. Tigers
can attain maturity in much
less than a year.
I comprehend of various that had
been in captivity for 12 years,
making them at
least thirteen years old. For most,
10 years is a right existence span.

CHAPTER 2

ACQUIRING A TIGER SALAMANDER

Some tiger salamanders are blanketed by way of law, the most important examples being the California tiger and the Sonoran tiger (A. mavortium stebbinsi). The Jap tiger is included in some states, such as New Jersey. California and New Jersey hinder the possession of any of the mole salamanders, so if you stay in both countries you nee d to reflect on consideration on any other salamander species as a pet. In addition, a number of states both restrict the possession or at least the sale of their state-native tigers. Tiger salamanders regularly grow to be obese, so it is essential to restrict meals such as wax worms to occasional treats. Despite their tame nature, tiger salamanders are notoriously tough to breed in captivity. All reviews of breeding have been carried out with aquatic (gilled) adults, hormone injections, or through preserving the salamanders in outside prerequisites for a whole lot of the year. Consequently, all tiger salamanders stored in captivity are of wild origin. This offers a restricted set of acquisition preferences for the budding tiger salamander enthusiast. If you have a kingdom fishing license and it is prison to accumulate and possess tigers in your state, one alternative is to seem for eggs or larvae (tadpoles) in ponds in the springtime. In many states you can accumulate tiger salamander larvae thru the bait fishing trade. They are regularly known as "water dogs," although now not all of the water puppies offered are simply tiger salamanders, so this is now not the most dependable source. Many reptile and amphibian companies have tigers on hand in late summertime and early fall, and these are typically newly metamorphosed juveniles. The gain of obtaining a metamorph is that you can commonly inform what race/subspecies of tiger you're acquiring. Buying larvae from the bait shop is something of a potluck, however most bait tigers are blotched or barred tigers.

CHAPTER 3

CARE AND HABITATON OF TIGER SALAMANDER

Tigers

are possibly the best salamanders

to house and care for in captivity.

However, the necessities of larvae

and terrestrial tigers are very

different.

If you've received a water dog, you

will want to maintain it aquatically

in the equal manner as the axolotl

Briefly, they require

a wholly aquatic setup with

clean, nonetheless water. If a filter is used, make positive to limit the electricity of outflow due to the fact these animals do now not tolerate strongly flowing water. When a larva starts to lose its tail fin, limit the water degree to barely cowl the salamander, and both supply an effortlessly available island or elevate the aquarium at one cease so the larva can effortlessly depart the water when it is ready. Like most amphibians, tigers can drown without difficulty at this precocious stage. Larval tigers ought to no longer be saved with fish, and ideally they ought to be saved in low numbers, for instance no extra than three giant larvae in a 10-gallon aquarium. This will limit leg and gill nipping, as properly as retaining feces and waste meals at a manageable level.

SEARCHING FOR WILD TIGER SALAMANDERS

Tiger salamanders of one race or every other are observed throughout the continental United States. They inhabit numerous habitats, such as the forests of the Pine Barrens on New Jersey's Atlantic Coast to the Sonoran Desert in Arizona. Despite their large distribution, they are hardly ever encountered by means of discipline herpetologists. In contrast, the "water dog" larva of the tiger salamander is regularly occurring to small boys and bass fishermen alike. The Llano Estacado, essentially an especially broad and lengthy desk mountain or "mesa", is the southern extension of the Great Plains, achieving south previous Lubbock, Texas and west over the border into New Mexico. To describe it as barren can also be an understatement.

There's surely no strolling water, and the temperature in the summer time soars into the 100s, solely to plummet beneath freezing in the snow-punctuated winter. In places, you can go for miles except seeing a single tree, and the arid land is so flat that you may want to be forgiven for questioning you can see the curvature of the Earth on the horizon. It's sincerely now not the first region you would seem for any amphibian, but shockingly, in this arid cowboy country, the barred tiger salamander (Ambystoma mavortium mavortium) is the most plentiful backboned animal by way of weight! Don't spend hot summer time nights searching for them — they solely come out in the rain. Perhaps greater than any different mole salamander, they spend their days and nights underground, frequently making use of the tunnels of the prairie canine cities that are the solely substantial facets on the landscape. But when the first heavy rains of March and April come, the horde emerges to tour to their breeding pools. All of the humans of

the location understand what a tiger salamander is due to the fact these massive amphibians

die by way of the lots on roads, or they quit up in homes via the gaps at the backside of doorways, on their way to their ponds. Tiger larvae can be caught in nets in the course of the spring, summer time and fall. Eastern tiger salamanders are high-quality determined in

late iciness or very early spring, as they ride to their breeding ponds. Unlike their extra westerly cousins, they don't have an explosive migration, and adults are mainly difficult to find. Eggs are regularly observed connected t o aquatic particles in small bunch of 50 to 200, and larvae can be fished up with nets in the course of the year.

CHAPTER 4

CAGING AND TEMPERATURE

Terrestrial/metamorphosed tiger salamanders are very straightforward. If you desire to make a show terrarium, reflect n consideration on the use of a large aquarium, at least 20 gallons in extent for two individuals. A 20 "long" aquarium is higher than a 20 "high" due to the fact the salamanders will now not use the vertical area supplied through mos t display aquariums. For non-display purposes, I like to use massive plastic storage boxes. My preferred minimal measureme nt for a tiger is a 58-quart, obvious plastic storage container handy at most massive supermarkets. Whether you use an aquarium or a storage box, a tight-fitting lid is necessary to forestall the salamanders from escaping. Large adults discover it very hard to get away aquariums and boxes, and indeed, once tame they hardly ever strive to do so, however having a lid or aquarium hood in vicinity is a sensible decision.

Being mole salamanders, tigers like to burrow. When first acquired, they have a tendency to spend most of their time buried in the substrate till feeding time. When deciding on a salamander substrate, I use a business topsoil combine bought from a hardware store. Be positive to buy one free of fertilizers and synthetic ingredients. Like all amphibians, salamanders have permeable skin and can take in toxins with no trouble from their surroundings. If you have got right of entry to to a backyard free of pesticides and herbicides, some other alternative is

to acquire your personal soil.   If
neither   of
these choices is accessible to   you,
a 0.33 alternative is to use coconut
fiber, now   and   again bought as
"coir," as a soil replacement such
as   the   Zoo   Med   Eco   Earth
Compressed   Coconut   Fiber
Expandable   Reptile   Substrate.
However, actual topsoil
and business topsoil
mixes provide an extra chemically
and
biologically steady surroundings t
han coconut fiber, and require a
lot much   less familiar changing.
These giant amphibians lunge for

their meals and often ingest particles of substrate. Small fragments of bark and fern fiber ought to probably lead to intestine impactions and the loss of life of your salamander. If the substrate you select incorporates giant parti cles, reflect on consideration on passing it thru some best wire mesh prior to use in the terrarium. Four inches of substrate must be regarded a mini mal depth. Deeper is better, from the tiger's factor of view. Wild tigers have been uncovered as a ways as 5 ft into the ground! The substrate ought to be spot cleaned

of   waste meals and   feces the
place possible,   and need
to be modified totally each three
to 4 months,   or extra many
times if you use coconut fiber.
Planted terrariums require whole
lot much   less prevalent substrate
maintenance, however tigers have
a   tendency to   uproot
and harm most   of
the standard terrarium plant
life in   the path of   their each
day digging. If you   do   use
plants, think   about the   usage
of larger, more   difficult plants,
such   as   pothos/devil's   ivy
(Epipremnum aureum), temperate
philodendrons,   or think

about synthetic silk plants. If you desire to maintain the tigers on the floor extra often, I discover the hides made from whole half-branches of timber to be excellent, like the Zoo Med Habba Hut. I've additionally observed a sheet of flat timber or even inflexible darkish plastic to be very popular. Simply lay it flat on the substrate and the tigers will dig a melancholy at once underneath. Lift the sheet and you'll typically be greeted through a hungry smile. Tigers will even excavate semi-permanent tunnels and take a seat simply interior with their heads poking out, ready for food. Sphagnum

moss, both residing and re-hydrated, is an exact addition to cowl the substrate's surface. It aids in maintaining moisture and appears as a substitute nice. Live temperate mosses such as the Flukers Live Moss can do properly in tiger terrariums if strategically positioned away from the predominant digging areas. Tigers do properly in a broad vary of humidity. As a common guideline, the substrate have to be moist, however if you squeeze

some in your arms it shouldn't drip. I like to furnish a moisture gradient by way of wetting one cease of the terrarium and leaving
the different quit pretty dry. You can additionally add a giant water bowl if desired; simply be certain it can be without problems entered and exited, like the Exo Terra X-Large Reptile Water Dish. Tigers make an addiction of defecating in water bowls, which can useful resource in maintaining the terrarium clean. Dechlorinated faucet water is appropriate for water bowls and

for retaining the substrate moist. Misting is unnecessary, however distilled water or reverse osmosis water are preferable for this motive due to the fact they won't depart residue on the terrarium glass. Tiger salamanders tolerate a broad vary of temperatures. They will be lively and keen to devour when stored at 50 to seventy five ranges Fahrenheit. Races that originate from areas of the United States of America of greater intense temperature variations, such as the barred tiger group, will

tolerate each
day temperatures properly into the
80s.   The greater heat-sensitive
races, such as Jap tigers from the
northeastern section of the U.S.,
will go through warmness stress if
subjected   to   temperatures
above eighty stages for   long,   and
supplemental
heating must be pointless for   any
race of tiger.

LIGHTING

Terrarium lights are no
longer required through salamand
ers. Despite being a nominally
nocturnal   animal,   I
have located adults lively in   the

wild all through the day. In captivity,
they appreciate no awesome night /day rule. New captives will regularly be cautious if subjected
to vibrant mild for lengthy interval s of time, however they have a tendency to overcome this alternatively quickly. Lighting the terrarium is in simple terms for the gain of any stay flowers in the enclosure and your viewing pleasure. If you are retaining plants,
make positive to use a plant-friendly bulb in the vary of 4,000 to 10,000 Kelvin (often offered as

being in the "daylight" or "freshwater" spectrum). Bulbs that emit giant quantities of warmth ar e satisfactory avoided, so think about a fluorescent fixture, such as these bought for aquariums, or even an LED lighting fixtures solution. The latter is an exceptional alternative if you do now not want to cater to light-hungry plants.

CHAPTER 5

FEEDING FOR TIGER SALAMANDER

New tigers will regularly spend lots of their time buried in the substrate, so you may additionally discover your self-having to dig your salamander out in order to feed it. As they come to be extra tame, they spend extra time on the floor and you won't have to dig as often. One feeding trick is to gently faucet the terrarium wall a few instances earlier than digging for the salamander or feeding these on the surface. Most tigers will study that the tapping is related with feeding time, and buried salamanders will normally emerge after a moment.

Like clearly all salamanders, tigers require no extra supplementation to their diet, so diet and mineral dusting is redundant.

An accurate staple meal with an occasional deal

with is flawlessly adequate.

Their fundamental weight-reduction plan in the wild is beetles, earthworms and crickets. In captivity, night crawlers are an extraordinary staple food, as are   crickets offered as stay reptile food.

Both ingredients are extraordinaril y low in fats and earthworms have an appropriate ratio of nutrients. Crickets must be intestine loaded with veggies and/or an industrial cricket eating regimen in order to enhance their nutrient   content. Another excellent staple   are captive-cultured cockroaches, such as   Blaptica   dubya. Tiger   salamanders frequently end up obese,   so   it is essential to restriction meals suc h as wax worms to occasional treats. Wax   worms   are without difficulty the preferred meals of tiger salamanders, and even the most reluctant tiger will locate it challenging to refuse them. It frequently helps to gently keep the wax worm with a forceps and rub it close to the nostril and on the mouth of the tiger. This is a specifically beneficial trick for newly captive tigers that are overly shy or skinny. Tigers will eat pinky and fuzzy mice with gusto, however these ingredients h ave tested to be particularly fattening and ought to solely be fed as a

very uncommon treat.
Perhaps extra than
any different amphibian,
tigers probable stumble
upon rodent nests in the wild.
Other deal
with ingredients encompasses mea
lworms,   Phoenix   worms,
hornworms,   silkworms,   and
even portions of   thawed   frozen
shrimp.
Larval   (gilled)   tigers   will
take comparable ingredients to
adults; however will additionally t
ake thawed/frozen bloodworms,
which are accessible at most pet
and   aquarium   stores.
Tigers have insatiable appetites.

Feed as a good deal as will be fed on with the aid of every tiger in 15 minutes. For adults, this generally ability two night crawlers. Adults need to be fed two to three instances per week at some stage in the hotter components of the year. You can limit this to as soon as each one or two weeks throughout wintry weather months if temperatures in the terrarium fall into the 50s. Juvenile tigers ought to be fed greater regularly, as frequently as each different day, due to the fact they are much less possibly to end

up overweight as
they dedicate the nutrients to
growth.

THE END